March

Shirley C. True

"The truly prudent man,
     who putteth himself aside,
Is like a tree growing
     in the garden;
He flourisheth and
     multiplieth his fruit;
He abideth in the presence
     of his lord;
His fruit is sweet;
     His shade is pleasant;
And he findeth his end in the
     garden."

—*Amenomope, 10th Century B.C.*

On Mockingbird Lake, dogwoods and Kurume azalea

Callaway Gardens:
The Unending Season

Text by Caleb Pirtle III
Southern Living Travel Editor

Photographs by Gerald Crawford
Southern Living Chief Photographer

Southern Living Books

Vice President and Director: Leslie B. Adams, Jr.
Editorial Director: John Logue
Marketing Director: David M. North
Book Editor: Betty Ann Jones

Callaway Gardens: The Unending Season

Text: Caleb Pirtle III
Photography: Gerald Crawford
Design: Philip T. Sankey
Editorial Assistants: Susanna Van Hoose, Karen Phillips, Carey Hinds

Library of Congress Catalog Card Number: 73-80502

Manufactured in the United States of America

First Printing 1973

Overleaf — Kurume azalea

Rhododendron

Prunifolia azalea, winter buds

In the Beginning

Callaway Gardens nestles quietly along the gentle foothills of Pine Mountain, sheltered and shadowed by the picturesque peaks of a timbered highland it calls home. It hides in springtime behind a flirting, flaming veil of azaleas and rhododendrons. Tiny, fragile wildflowers fight their way through the thick, winter carpet of leaf mold to lazily pass the days of summer, nodding and bowing as if in agreement with the whispers of the wind, waiting to fade away with the promised frost that comes to lacquer autumn fire on the leaves of the forest.

The mountains of the Piedmont of Georgia were old when man found them, antiqued by too many yesterdays, and rounded by the coming of the winds and the pounding of the rains. This last, stubborn foothold of the Appalachians holds the rare distinction of being the oldest range of mountains in North America, perhaps in the northern hemisphere. They were ancient and beaten down and respected when the terrain that one day would become the Rockies was still flat and sandy and monotonous.

But because the Piedmont Appalachians have had such a long evolutionary history, valuable time has been earned, then spent, developing the largest number of plant species in the world. And with the wearing down of the mountains, a greater variety of natural habitats has been created in the flatlands, the creek bottoms, the timbered ravines. Climates fluctuate from very moist to very dry, from very cold to very hot on neighboring hillsides.

In fact, in those tucked away, protected valleys grow plants that seem to be, at first glance, wandering lost and astray from the coastal tropics. Yet only a few hundred yards away, in rocky areas and sand pits, you can find, herded together in thorny patches, prickly pear, a cactus whose relatives thrive in the arid Southwestern desert. They are living in harmony, side by side, on the shadowed floor of an old, old land.

This became the land of Cason Callaway, a man who knew that the woods are made for the hunters of dreams . . . that gardens were born before gardeners . . . that nature can sometimes use a helping hand.

It was on a ridge overlooking the old Barnes Creek Watershed near Hamilton, Georgia, that fate reached out and tapped Cason Callaway. The year was 1930.

He was alone when he stumbled across a flowering shrub. It didn't have just ordinary flowers, but was a unique and puzzling species of azalea. He had never seen one quite like it before, and it would be a plant he would never forget.

Callaway snapped off a flower, took it home, and gave it to his wife, Virginia, a knowledgeable horticulturist, a delicate woman who felt right at home with the woodland. Callaway had once been described as a completely practical businessman. Yet he would often follow his wife as she slipped along those quiet forest paths, watching as she would gingerly tend to each plant — no matter how small or ragged. And he sought to share her appreciation of nature.

Virginia identified the unusual blossom as a prunifolia azalea (*Rhododendron prunifolium*), a sensitive woodland flower, the colors of orange and red, that blooms in midsummer and early autumn, long after the other native azaleas have lost their springtime blush.

Prunifolia azalea

Callaway learned it was a shrub so rare that it was found nowhere else on earth except in a few scattered drifts within a 100-mile radius or so of Blue Springs, the water that flowed into old Barnes Creek.

Virginia Callaway remembers: "The decision to buy Blue Springs on the Barnes Creek property was influenced by the discovery of that prunifolia azalea. But what ultimately led to the creation of the Gardens was Cason's desire to share the natural beauty of his section of Pine Mountain especially with the citizens of Harris County. He also felt that it could be an inspirational asset to Georgia, the whole nation, and even visitors from overseas.

"In all that he did with the Gardens he insisted on top quality because he said he wanted it so beautiful that it would make visitors want to go home and hang their pictures of life higher on the wall."

So Callaway, in that August of 1930, bought his first parcel of land at Blue Springs. He and Virginia would picnic there; it became their place of escape from those telephones that kept ringing on Sunday afternoons. He brought friends with him, and together they would walk the quiet woodland, trekking across the pine straw that matted the hillside floor around Barnes Creek.

Kurume azalea

And Callaway sought to save the prunifolia azalea. If this plumleaf azalea was a vanishing species that still called his Georgia "home," then Callaway was not about to waste valuable time that could be spent in ensuring its future.

He employed a man to wander into the heart of his forestland to seek out the rare azalea and to collect its seeds. What he had in mind was to grow enough of this beautiful, wild azalea so that it might never wither away and be lost to the ages — never be reduced to a memory that was beyond being relived.

The seeds — 20,000 of them — were gathered, tenderly germinated, and the seedlings carefully planted beside the bubbling waters of Blue Springs. Five years later they bloomed. And one day they would be moved to form the nucleus of an eden called Callaway Gardens.

For the next 20 years, while Callaway walked among the wildflowers and along trails of native azalea and dogwood, he discovered that much of the natural beauty remaining in this Piedmont land had been hidden away in ravines too deep for man or sawmills to destroy. Once, back before the turn of the century, cotton had sapped the soil and erosion had cut ugly scars across the misused farmland. However, the terrain, when Callaway came, had as nature willed, already begun the long, tough fight — the valiant struggle to reclaim itself. It was a battle Callaway was eager to join.

What must be done, he reasoned, was to bring life back to the surrounding countryside and weave it like a master craftsman into those widespread and orphan patches of native flora, onto those pineywood hillsides that had managed to survive the wrath of cotton pickers marching through Georgia. Then, future generations would find something more in the trees and stones and brooks than they could ever learn in books or ever discover in the words of a teacher.

The time had come to tie down the hills that had begun to rapidly wash and slide away, to throw up an ecological roadblock of plants against the scars of erosion, and to carefully and scientifically cultivate the lowlands to make them fertile again. Upon those worn slopes were planted acres of crops to hold the soil together. The bottomlands, choked and bogged down with silt, were drained. And those nutrient-hungry pasturelands were woven with alfalfa and clover to restore their fertility.

Cluster of bluets

*Bumblebee on
crab apple branch*

Callaway had once said, "You can put a 10-cent flower in a 50-cent hole and it will live and grow and thrive. But if you put a 50-cent flower in a 10-cent hole, it will die."

He had begun the long process of helping nature reclaim its birthright, bringing back that forgotten, misplaced heritage that had been stolen from the environment by the agricultural misuse of the soil so many, many years before. He said, "Every child ought to see something beautiful before he's six years old — something he will remember all his life."

The idea for a garden, perhaps, had been planted that day beside old Barnes Creek Watershed. It would take time for the idea to take root and grow and develop. But then it always does. And in the end it would bud for a while, then burst into bloom across 2,500 acres in the valley of Pine Mountain.

The creation and completion of the blueprint would have taken more than two decades. But time was insignificant because it would be the last, great, benevolent project Callaway could leave proudly behind him. He even told his son, "Bo, we don't want to just build the finest garden seen on earth since Adam was a boy. What we want to do is build the prettiest garden that will ever be seen on earth 'til Gabriel blows his horn."

In order to help transform these woodland gullies and terraced hillsides into a great garden, Fred Galle was engaged as director of horticulture. It would be his ultimate responsibility to make the gardens grow naturally and realistically, to blend the imported with the native vegetation and give it the welcome appearance of rightfully belonging there all along. It would not be an easy task. But it would happen in the end just as Callaway always knew it would.

Galle remembers, "We hoped to do in 20 years what it would normally take nature, working alone, two centuries to accomplish."

As Callaway firmly believed: "The earth is the Lord's and the people who claim certain parts of it hold only a temporary title. And for what land they hold, they one day will have to give an account."

This then is the story of Callaway Gardens—the land and its rebirth — a charming kind of place for all seasons where you can escape to the backcountry, search for a fleeting glimpse of serenity, and find the hollows where the flowers grow.

Callaway Gardens was opened in May of 1952. It was an era when Callaway reasoned, "Rich men can always find a place of beauty to go to, but it's the factory worker or salesman — everyman — who, with but limited funds, needs a place to go with his family for a happy quiet stay in beautiful surroundings."

He said, "If a man wanted to take his kids swimming, all that was available to him was a muddy frog pond. If he wanted to take his family on a picnic, the best place he could find was a cut-over forest of pine stumps."

The pine stumps are still there, nestled along the old terraces and hedgerows that rise up as grim reminders of yesterday's plow. They've been overshadowed now by the towering trunks of the loblolly pines, reaching stoically above the damp banks of the creek bottoms. The pines umbrella the hilly terrain like great evergreen canopies sewn together against the sky by the needles of their own branches.

The hardwoods are returning, slowly taking a stronger foothold on hillsides where man is dedicated to preserving their existence, rather than threatening to end it. Blackjack oak and hickories and southern pine cling steadfastly to the sun-dappled hillsides.

White oak, chestnut oak, dogwood, and sourwood hover together on the moist northern slopes, a corner of the Piedmont where the sun seldom finds its way. And down along the creeks, the sweetgum, the stately tulip poplar, and red maple join the loblolly pine, always at home beside the creeping waters of a sunken swamp.

Fred Galle points out, "Our major focus in the Garden is on native material, from dogwoods to mountain laurel to native azaleas. We wanted to use and preserve these plants and wildflowers and trees in their natural setting, to bring many of these species back to their homeland, and reintroduce them into their own accepted plant communities.

"Then to increase the impact of this scenic beauty, we added hundreds of indigenous plants, while in the informal areas we've imported plants from all parts of the United States and from abroad.

"When the project really got under way back in the early days of the 50's, the trees in the area were predominantly pine. Now they are changing gradually to hardwood with new forests of white and red oak up on the dry ridges, as well as Florida maple, southern sugar maple, black gum, hickory, and tulip poplar.

Coral Bell, Kurume azalea

"And, of course, it's always gratifying to watch the development of the dogwood and redbuds, to see them adding color back in the dark inner sanctum of the forest."

All Callaway and Galle had done was to give nature a boost, to lend a helping hand. They didn't want to wait two centuries before the forests could stand with pride again. Two decades or less, they decided, was long enough.

During those first 15 years, more than 10,000 permanent trees and shrubs were planted annually. Holly and magnolia collections were started. There were walking paths laced with the vibrant hybrid rhododendrons.

Slopes were christened and covered with banks of myrtle and bay, surrounded by wild hydrangeas, mountain laurel, sweet shrub, ferns and gentians, wild roses, grancy graybeard, crab apple and plum, dogwood and redbud. Gardens, special and beckoning, were landscaped for roses and chrysanthemums.

Then the azaleas came, the royalty of Callaway flora. Thirty-five hundred white, fragrant arborescens azaleas were transplanted; hundreds of the rare prunifolia — the plumleaf azalea — direct descendants of Callaway's surprising discovery those many years ago — were brought in and laid like rich, fine carpet across Georgia's hillsides. Five hundred different species and varieties of azaleas now live in the Gardens, making it one of the largest collections in the country.

Tiny streams, that once were useful only to transport fallen leaves on a spinning journey to little ponds far back in the timberlands, have been dammed and lakes are sprawling through the heart of the forest, their channels reaching like long ladyfingers into the narrow ravines and natural coves that lean down close to the water's edge.

12

Mountain Creek Lake was the first, built by Callaway long before the opening of the Gardens, originally created solely as a hideaway refuge for his friends to enjoy. It is also the largest lake (175 acres) at the Gardens and has been fertilized and stocked with bream and bass, proving, as Callaway knew it eventually would, that an acre of water, if handled properly, could be worth more than an acre of land.

There are 13 lakes now, spreading like tranquil mirrors back into the frontyard of mountains, reflecting abstractly the giant trees that cast their shadowed images across the wind-rippled water. Coots paddle playfully into the shelter of the coves. Mallards drift lazily like feathered buoys. Pine needles float downward from overhanging limbs, nestle softly onto the surface, and begin their journey with the wind toward shore. Fishing and boating are permitted only on Mountain Creek Lake. The remaining dozen lakes have been saved to reflect the peacefulness and serenity of a gentle forest.

The summer winds of 1952 had escorted June into the Appalachians and the landscape was in full bloom when Callaway, recuperating from eye surgery, was driven past that big front gate in the old familiar grey Cadillac. He had missed the opening ceremonies. But now he was headed toward home in Blue Springs. It was there that they brought him the news. During those first 10 days 4,308 fishermen had crowded down to the banks of Mountain Creek Lake and had taken out 8½ tons of bass and bream. The largest bass weighed almost 9 pounds. And that made him happy. For the aging Callaway had always vowed, "We don't own the Gardens. We just kind of work here. They belong to all who enjoy them."

And so the Gardens were endowed and placed in the care of the non-profit Ida Cason Callaway Foundation. They offer more than just a pilgrimage to the world of azalea and rhododendron and

Sweet azalea, winter buds

Flicker on lightpost

Bordering 15th fairway, Kurume azaleas

Hinomayo, Kurume azalea

dogwood. There is golf. Tennis. Horseback trails meandering back into the timbered mountains. The world's largest man-made beach. A miniature fleet of paddle boats and canoes. Trap and skeet shooting. A quail hunting preserve. Rustic cottages scattered in a pine woodland. And a resort inn, specializing in homemade biscuits, muscadine jam, speckled heart grits, and country ham.

During summer, circus comes to Callaway Gardens, the fast-paced product of Florida State University. In winter the Southern Highlands Handicraft Guild conducts arts and crafts exhibitions, demonstrating the old-fashioned, hand-me-down skills of spinning, weaving, pottery making, and leather crafts.

Throughout the year, horticultural workshops provide the gardener with a first-hand living experience with flowers. Those enrolled are generally handed tools and a pot and plant; given instruction on cutting, trimming, and fertilizing; then allowed to carry flowers home with them to watch their handiwork grow.

Once each year, Callaway Gardens salutes the heritage of another country. It began in the 1960's when Mrs. Virginia Callaway returned from an excursion through the famous tulip fields of Holland. She suggested a foreign festival annually to "focus attention on flowers from abroad." Her idea has now been expanded to emphasize the chosen country's customs, its traditions, and its culture.

Yet the emphasis, as it has always been, is on the Gardens themselves — the land Cason Callaway came to heal.

With the Gardens open, Callaway was no longer just a hunter of dreams. As he had wished, every man now had a quiet, gentle place to come to. The trees and the wildflowers, teased and toyed by the breezes, would gather him in like family.

And come man did — 57,492 that first year.

There are 63 holes of golf to welcome him. When the sport was introduced into the valley of the pines, those first nine fairways were carved into the forest with one thought in mind: "To make it extremely difficult for an amateur duffer to lose a ball." Then, as a final touch, the roughs were shaved barber-smooth. They have been carefully designed for the golfer who hates to "half-lose" a golf ball, the kind who wants to find his slice, shank, or hook quickly or to know it is gone forever into the water or the woods.

It became the Gardens' philosophy that whenever a golfer made the mistake of lifting his head on a shot, he should be able to see something beautiful. So the lakes and the fairways were bordered with woodland plants and shrubs and magnolia trees — a bit of floral lace in the foreground of the mountains.

The 63 holes are more of a challenge now for the golfers who play 106,000 rounds here each year. The hungry lakes claim more than their rightful share of misguided balls, and the roughs are rougher; the woodland thicket is slowly creeping down closer to the edge of the fairways.

Tommy Aaron, 1973 champion of the prestigious Masters Golf Tournament, calls Callaway Gardens his home base. He knows the courses well.

Aaron says, "The Mountain View course is more to the taste of the tournament player or the fellow who's looking for a challenge. You can play the championship tees there and stretch it out to 7,040 yards or play the reds and bring it down to the club player distance of 6,605 yards. From the ladies' tees, it's still 5,834 yards.

"Lake View is the oldest, a sporty kind of course that appeals to the vacation player. He's the type of golfer who likes to go home and tell his friends about a good score. He can score better on Lake View.

"The most scenic hole, the fifth hole, furnishes one of the most familiar and traditional golfing scenes in America. It is a 150-yard hole that crosses a lake. And it's all carry over water, playing toward that picturesque old clubhouse." Now, it's the Gardens Restaurant.

Blueberry

Clubhouse —now Gardens Restaurant

Piedmont azalea, native

Moss and lichens on chestnut rail
of old log cabin

Winter squash in oak basket

Mallards

Oconee azalea, winter flower buds

American holly seedling

Wild plum branch

Nestled at the foot of the mountain, gazing out across the 14th green, the clubhouse brings to the Gardens a touch of 17th century England with its Provincial style, its hand-hewn oak beams, and its hand-rived shingles. And that's only proper, not really so out of place at all. For wasn't it over the rolling hills of Scotland where they first really began playing this maddened game called golf?

Aaron continues: "On any of the three 18-hole courses you've got that mountain range for a backdrop. But as you play Gardens View, you find yourself among the vineyards, where the grapes are growing, that eventually go into the Gardens' famous preserves. The environment is sort of Aegean, I suppose you would say."

Golf isn't the only sport at Callaway Gardens where water is the creator of the great challenge. During July each year, the calm, unruffled surface of Robin Lake churns with the explosive umbrella wakes of the country's premier water skiing tournament: the Masters Championship.

And from June through August, the Florida State University Circus flies beneath the big top of a red and yellow and white candy-striped tent, perched in an open field just beyond the modernistic pavilion of Robin Lake. This is the stage for what has been rightfully called the "Greatest Collegiate Show on Earth," the summer home for the FSU Circus.

But students don't just spend their time in the sawdust arena, weaving among the spider web of yellow ropes and lines and rigging, or sailing on the trapeze above a net that waits for them to fall. They also supervise activities for both children and adults, ranging from arts and crafts to drama, music, golf, tennis, archery, swimming, water skiing, dancing, and, of course, circus performing. Children not only have a learning experience, but they also identify with the performers. The man who taught them to water ski is suddenly flying 30 feet above the sawdust.

23

Bordering Mockingbird Lake,
Kurume azaleas — Sherwood Red and Snow

Far from the madding crowd of circus fever, there stands in silence, a lone monument to another day. It huddles back among the black gum trees of the Meadowlark area of the Gardens: an authentic, unpainted log cabin, beaten by the winds and rains and dating back to the mid-1800's. It is open daily from 9 a.m. to 5 p.m.

Five board steps lead steeply to an old wooden porch. The shutters on the windows are open and the surrounding trees are reflected brightly in the wavy glass panes, looking much as their reflections would in the mirrored surface of a calm mountain lake.

We open the rusted iron latch and hear a hostess, dressed in a long, frilly gingham dress of the 19th century, say, "Well, come on in before the wind blows you through the front door."

The hostess smiles and tells us that the cabin had been built by slave labor in the early 1800's about 20 miles away in Troup County, near LaGrange. "It was found one day in 1959. Owen L. Riley, the chief forest consultant for this region, was out rambling through a thickly wooded section of the forest and accidentally stumbled across the old cabin.

"He told Mr. Callaway about it — the Gardens were only seven years old at the time. And you know Mr. Callaway. He was always on the lookout for something interesting as well as educational.

"All of the logs are hand-hewn, and some are almost 2 feet thick. They tell me somebody lived in the old cabin until 1936. So, you see, it's had a long and useful existence."

They combed the · countryside, the hostess said, searching for authentic antiques that would feel comfortable and not look out of place in the one-room cabin. Gradually, piece by piece, the house — abandoned two decades earlier — began to look more and more like a home.

A Dutch oven that cooked all meals over an open fire and a black iron pot for vegetables and stews hang beside the fireplace. Nearby is the dishrag gourd used to scrub them.

There is a dough tray for biscuits and a dough chest with that third compartment to hold Georgia grits. And on the wall beside it is an old, old looking glass. Its owners, now unknown and forgotten, so many years ago had decoupaged the wooden frame with flowers clipped from a seed catalog.

Hanging from a spice rack above the mantel where they had been left to dry are herbs and spices: rosemary, oregano, sweet basil, lemon basil, and dill. And left open beside the bed, in its due place of respect, is the family Bible, printed in Old English in 1791 in Massachusetts. Its faded pages have been turned to the Psalm:

"Behold, how good and how pleasant it is for brethren to dwell together in unity."

It is as Hal Northrop, president of the Gardens, told us, "Cason Callaway wanted so desperately for the people of the area to hang their picture of life a little higher on the wall. In our world today, we do too much too fast. Callaway wanted a place where man could pause for a moment and reflect on the goodness of the world around him, stand alone and meditate if he so desired in the quietness of the forest, a place of peace where his search for serenity could end.

"A refuge for escape in today's world is important. In tomorrow's world, it will be even more important."

Refuge. And escape. The undying symbol of this profound belief is the Ida Cason Callaway Memorial Chapel, a small sanctuary rising up beside tranquil Falls Creek Lake as though it — like the forest around it — just grew there from a seed planted in the valley.

It is English Gothic, reflected in the waters of the small lake, and designed after the rural wayside chapels of the 16th and 17th centuries. Native quartzite fieldstones, gathered from surrounding fields, were used for its walls and those massive red oak beams came out of Georgia forests. The floor is Cherokee flagstone from North Georgia, and the huge altar stone typifies the many boulders that perch on the antique slopes of Pine Mountain.

The four windows facing west are of stained glass, and each represents a season of the year. The first features the dogwood and azaleas of spring; the second highlights the green leaves of the hardwood and the flowers of summer; the third depicts the reds and yellows and oranges, the hues that frost has lacquered on autumn trees; and the last window pays tribute to the hollies and the evergreens that bring color to the stark winter greyness of the woodland.

Pine forests are etched on the large window to the south, and the window facing north picks up the splashes and leaf patterns of a hardwood forest that is making its comeback in the Piedmont.

Outside, a small trail slips among the clusters of mountain laurel and dogwood and native azaleas. And on the afternoons of every Sunday, you can hear the music of a Moller pipe organ as it plays from a bell-toned tower in the chapel — a concert to the woods and all who gather there.

Sweetgum, new leaves

Ida Cason Callaway Memorial Chapel

Snow, Kurume azalea

Florida azalea, native

Watchful grey squirrel on pine

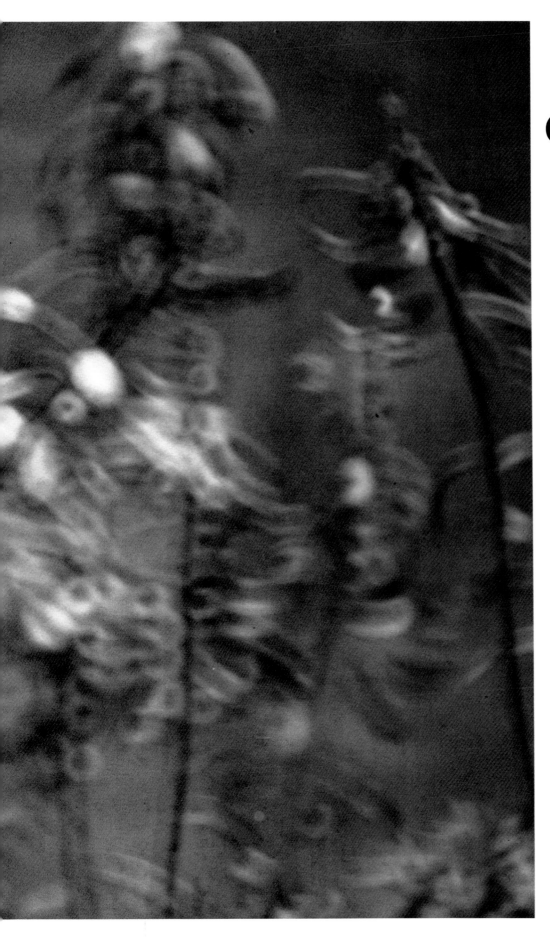

The
Hidden
Gardens

It is winter.

The leaves are gone, underfoot now, and the trees are holding their bare grey branches upward as if in a long, silent prayer for the coming of spring. The ground is a patchwork rug of packed brown leaves, dried and brittle, cracking and popping beneath the crunching of your footsteps.

It is a friendly sound, much like the beckoning crackle of a woodburning fireplace when the frost has melted from the logs. Only the evergreens are clothed, bending their limbs slightly against the brisk rustling of a wind that swings easily from tree to tree, then blows away in perpetual anonymity across the lakes.

The backdrop of the naked forest is a stark grey. Callaway Gardens is an "environmental education center," one that gives you an opportunity to understand nature on its own terms by walking the pathways of its hidden gardens, by listening to the faraway cries of a bird in flight, and by living, for a time, with only the comfort of a forest to lean on.

Already a miniature sign of life has begun to awaken and climb shyly out of the leafy floor. The economy of nature is especially visible during late winter. With the trees still leafless and the warmer sunshine beginning to strike the forest floor, the green shoots of hundreds of small plants burst from the soil and raise their leaves skyward.

Most of these plants rush to develop their flowers and set their seed before the shade created by new leaves makes the environment unfavorable for their growth in late spring.

This is the time when the forest floor awakens and begins to tingle with life that will be invisible during the summer. The many seeds that are produced ensure continued life for next year and provide an abundance of food material for the countless small animals scurrying through the leaves and twigs.

In this way, nature permits a variety of plants and animals to flourish when it appears that the forest is dormant. This seasonal exchange of plant groups is one of the many ways in which nature makes it possible for many life forms to inhabit the same locality without directly competing with one another for precious nutrients. In March, there will be a tremendous rush of activity on the forest floor. Then the trees' leaves will sprout out and shade the little plants. The sun will be cut off. And the plants will wither away and die, leaving their seeds for tomorrow.

The long, long sleep will begin.

At Mountain Creek Lake Dam, the spillway is dotted with a frantic, solid covering of grackles and red wing blackbirds, hopping tiptoe, it seems, in the shallow sheet of rushing water that is hurrying back into the woodland.

Dew on Johnson grass

Fruit of possumhaw holly

Junco on spillway near Mountain Creek Lake

In the distance, a flock of robins, appearing cocky and satisfied and almost too fat to fly, are again attacking the last of the season's red holly berries. The yellow berries are virtually untouched and untasted. For some strange, unexplainable reason, the birds will deliberately wait until no red berries are left before finally turning to the tiny yellow fruit.

With the coming of early spring, all the robins will get together again for that long flight northward, leaving the berries that are left for the cedar waxwings. They will relish the leftovers with unwarranted gratitude.

More than 450 varieties of hollies spotlight the five meandering holly trails that twist like their corkscrew leaves back among the anchoring pine trees of the Meadowlark area. Three are American holly trails, and there is one pathway each for English and Oriental hollies. Walking time for each trail is about 15 minutes.

In winter when most trees — other than the ever-present pine — have nothing to display but their bare, unwrapped limbs, the holly suddenly accepts the starring floral role of the Georgia woodland, much like the talented understudy who spends most of his life awaiting that one break which will shove him into the applause of center stage.

The American holly is traditionally thought of as a pyramidal tree with dull, olive green, spiny leaves and red berries. However, many varied forms, such as the spineless leaf and yellow-fruited hybrids, are also on the trail, standing irregularly like hitchhikers in a strange land.

Other species, with fallen, brown pine needles hanging from their stems like misplaced Christmas decorations, include the black-fruited inkberry, the white-fruited gallberry, Foster holly, and yaupon hollies which are large, dwarfed, yellow-fruited, or even weeping.

The English holly, lovely though it may be, is too stubborn, it sometimes seems, to even make a halfhearted effort to grow up. It is noted for its glossy foliage, its numerous, variegated leaves and its red, orange, and yellow berries.

Dawn redwood

Raindrops on bald cypress branch

But English hollies are less tolerant to warm summer temperatures and subsequently are virtually unknown in the South. They require, more than anything else perhaps, a great deal of patience.

Ben Pace, assistant director of horticulture for the Gardens, remembers apologizing one afternoon to an important visitor from England. He said, "I'm afraid our English holly is not doing very well. The soil and the climate are just not right."

The Englishman only shrugged. "That's all right," he answered. "It grows slowly in England, too. You see, it's a lifelong challenge to get the holly to grow properly. Those magnificent bushes you see over in England have been tenderly cared for for centuries."

The Oriental holly trail has a multitude of species from China, Japan, and their neighboring islands. These hollies have quickly become extremely popular in landscaping.

The Japanese holly is widely grown and is usually characterized by its small spineless leaves and black fruit. And, above all, it can be totally unpredictable. Some of the carefully labeled "dwarf Japanese hollies" found in nurseries suddenly grow up to be towering, green giants.

Chinese holly is typified by its glossy foliage and large, red berries. It is best-known by its spineless, leaved form, commonly called Burford. Along the Gardens' 5-mile drive, near the Lakeview Golf Course clubhouse, the winding roadside is bordered like lace with these magnificent Burford hollies, climbing upward 20 to 30 feet.

But back along the self-guided trail, your footpath is lined with such species as longstalk holly, lusterleaf holly, pernyi holly, and saw-tooth holly, the early bird that begins to bring its red berries out proudly in August.

Hollies, even on their own special trails, never have to stand alone. For they share their color with a supporting cast led by those spreading drifts of daffodils, nodding like silent, yellow bells in the afternoon breeze, and calling on the yew, the plum yew, and Chinese fir for an evergreen backdrop.

The English holly trail blends easily with the blooms of the pyracantha, tea plant, dwarf and common nandina, photinia, and the cotoneasters.

And rising mightily upward from the trail, as though they are resurrected monuments to another age — to a forgotten era — are the rare dawn redwood trees. Until the 1940's when America was at war, the dawn redwood was only known by its fossilized remains, a tree that most people believed had not managed to survive the unpredictability of the centuries — a remnant that men could only speak of with question marks, then spend hours wondering and speculating and trying to reconstruct the ecological reasons for its disappearance.

Suddenly the mystery ended.

Shrouded in secrecy, a military expedition under the guise of scientific exploration stumbled into an isolated valley in the mountains of Tibet. There they found the lost dawn redwood growing in such widespread abundance that it was actually being lumbered.

One of the scientists brought back some of the seeds and a prominent national arboretum began the careful, painstaking recovery of the rare tree in the United States. It was discovered that the missing dawn redwood literally grew in leaps and bounds. And some of those trees, grown from the original seeds and planted but a mere two decades ago, now stand with pride, 80 feet tall.

The tree with the chartreuse leaf, lost over the centuries, has returned.

Evergreen barberry, mahonia, the Zabel laurel, and the tea olive add to the floral arrangement of the American holly trail, along with Alexandria laurel, used symbolically by Alexander the Great as he tried desperately not only to conquer, but also to unite the world.

And weaving throughout the Oriental holly trail, you will find the mystical bloom in early September of the spider lily.

We walked away from the cluster of holly, leaving the berries (both red and yellow) to the robins and a cantankerous, noisy bluejay that kept zipping rather rudely into the needled pointed branches to eat his own food, or steal from another bird, whichever, at the moment, seemed the easiest and wisest thing to do. Then, in a sudden splash of faded, winter blue, the jay was gone; the forest became quiet again, secure in the bosom of its own living things, including those tiny buds gripping the ends of azalea limbs that had not yet been fed enough sunshine to burst into life.

Galle and his staff had gone to work, as far back as 1954, to hybridize many of the native azaleas, using, also, some of the large, flowered and deciduous hybrids. They successfully crossed the Ghent hybrid Narcissiflora, the mollis hybrid Hugo Koster, and several others with the adaptable Southern species.

Galle said, "The culture of native azaleas is not difficult. In fact, they are among the easiest shrubs to grow, but they should be planted in some shade.

"However, in the past, the general trend has been for collectors to dig them bareroot or with small balls and sell them on the open markets of larger cities. Unless given special treatment, such as cutting back and 'babying' for a couple of years, these often die during that first season. Unless the plants are nursery-grown, poor survival can generally be expected."

On a wooded slope just east of the Overlook parking area, the famed Azalea Trail darts quickly down the hillside, rambling slowly into the crease of a leaf-patched ravine, overshadowing the velvet faces of cyclamen, Christmas roses, and sleeping wild ginger that look up from the bases of trees.

Perhaps the prize of the trail is the Kurume hybrid, an evergreen azalea that boasts white, pink, or red flowers. In spring, the forest is ablaze with color of Hinode-giri, Coral Bells, Pink Pearl, Snow, Salmon Beauty, and Christmas Cheer. Southern Indian azaleas, frequently displayed in gardens of the Deep South and along the Gulf Coast, have been mass planted along the trail, although they sometimes lose their floral buds if the weather has been unusually cold. The Satsuki hybrids, with colors ranging from white to deep red to lavender, usually flower in May. Satsuki means fifth month.

Just beyond the sprawling stand of hollies, at the crossroads of the Meadowlark area, native azaleas also decorate the celebrated Wildflower Trail as it faithfully follows a shallow, clear stream that comes bubbling out of the ridges of the woodland. But, alas, many of these native azaleas have, for years, been mistakenly referred to as bush honeysuckle or wild honeysuckle. Yet they, like all azaleas, belong wholeheartedly to the genus *Rhododendron.*

Mud turtle

White-tailed deer in woodland

Burford Chinese holly berries

Leaf of Osmanthus fortunei *shrub*

The Florida azalea usually heralds the advent of the flowering season in late March and early April. The oconee azalea, with blooms varying from salmon red to strong pink to yellow, has also spent much of its life on the Piedmont, veiled in confusion. Oldtimers erroneously called it the flame azalea. But the true flame azalea *(Rhododendron calendulaceum)*, also found along the padded footpath is the one that John Bartram, the famous Philadelphia botanist, described as "the most gay and brilliant flowered shrub yet known. It is the most celebrated species, with flowers the color of the finest red lead, orange, and bright gold, as well as yellow and cream."

Native azaleas merely add the window dressing to the Wildflower Trail. Its real character, and sometimes camouflaged beauty, is found in the tiny petals of plants that creep up through the covering of leaf mold, searching for the sunrays that ricochet downward from the branches of the oak, the tulip poplar, and the pine.

They are not always immediately visible — these newborn plant shoots — yet they wander there like lonely tin maidens waiting through the seasons for the return of their lonely tin soldiers. Some wither away, and their vigil in the valley is passed on to other flowers when their time on earth has ended for a season.

Life never ceases on the woodland floor, even when the trees are stark and grey — the ashen mask of winter. Nothing ever stands still in the forest.

On a knoll at the side of the road, the mountain laurel (or the calico bush) is one of the best of the native broadleaf evergreens, but poisonous if eaten. In late spring, when the flowers lift their pure, white and rose-pink heads, they watch the

Flower of wild ginger

coming of the bees in search of nectar. The flowers have ten pouches in which the anthers are inserted just prior to the pollen release. The frantic little insects release the anthers and a shower of pollen is flipped onto their backs for them to carry patiently on to the next bloom.

Circles of Christmas fern hover about the ground like gentle, green pinwheels. They are generally found in moist, shady locales, ruling quietly as the aging grandfathers of the forest. For these are ferns that existed on earth centuries before the appearance of any larger flowering plants. Legend has it that they were the one flower that failed to bloom the night Christ was born, and have been cursed to never bloom again.

A series of waterfalls races down a rock-strewn staircase, playing a splashing concerto to the gathering of the woods. The trees listen silently and respectfully, as an audience should, nodding their heads and limbs and branches with the gentle rhythm of the wind. Only the sound of the water can be heard as it rushes from nowhere in particular to nowhere in particular, and seems to be in such a hurry to get there. Pine cones, grey and thorny, lie among the fallen leaves, forgotten by the giant trees that shed them, wet in an early morning dew and glistening with the sparkle of costume jewelry.

The sweet shrub, smelling of spice and sporting dark reddish-brown flowers, has been associated with gardens since colonial days. It grows abundantly in rich woods and clearings throughout the Southland. In autumn, when its blooms have faded and died and blown away, the sweet shrub forms large, fig-shaped seedpods which often offer protective housing for spiders and insects as they flee the coming chill of winter. And when the leaves, too, are gone, these seedpods resemble dozens of brown cocoons just waiting for the warmth of spring to call them. It is a useful plant, the sweet shrub. Its brown seeds provide food for wildlife; its flowers are often placed in linen drawers, along with those seedpods collected in fall; and when the olden days were called good, its bark was used for medicinal purposes.

Waterfall on Wildflower Trail

Rue anemone

Trout lily

Periwinkle

Liverleaf

Lenten rose

Viburnum

Bloodroots

The devil's walking stick, sometimes known as the hercules club, is a strange plant, a small tree whose leaves are possibly larger than those of any other tree native to the Eastern United States. A single compound leaf may grow up to 4 feet long and 2 to 3 feet wide. In late summer, it has clusters of small, white flowers, replaced in early autumn by dark blue, juicy berries, awaiting the first of the southward flights of migratory birds. The crooked, spiny trunk, with unbranched stems, can easily be said to resemble a walking stick, thus the reason for its name.

The tulip tree, or yellow poplar, is growing straight, unwavering and unbending, toward the heavens. At its feet is coiled the downy rattlesnake orchid. And on its strong, grey trunk clings a patch of resurrection fern. When the days are dry, it turns brown and begins to shrivel away, but when the rains come, it pops out bright and green and proud again, as though it had never even thought of wasting away in famine.

The wildflower has no boundaries. It has its own trail, but it salts and peppers the paths of the Azalea Trail as well, and the Laurel Springs Trail, a short 700-yard walk through a typical lower Appalachian hardwood forest.

The brown-spotted trout lily ushers in spring. The bloodroot is white and fragile and closes in the hush of the evening; its roots and stems produce a brilliant acrid orange-scarlet juice used by southern Indians for painting and dyeing. The bluets are dainty and petite, and members of the same plant family as coffee and quinine; they huddle in colorful colonies and are sometimes called Quaker-ladies or innocence. The May-apple, usually in thickets and pastures, has edible fruit when ripe, but other parts of the plant are poisonous.

The wild geranium has seeds that look much like birds' beaks; in fact, the name "geranium" comes from the Greek word for the bird we know as a crane.

Jack-in-the-pulpit, found in moist woods and near stream beds, is considered poisonous if eaten raw; yet the American Indian boiled the turnip-shaped root for food. Mountain people took the fairy wand and made a tincture of the leaves for medicine.

Liverwort *(Hepatica)*, according to the Doctrine of Signatures of the Middle Ages, was a good cure for diseases of the liver. The cardinal flower is a favorite of the ruby-throated hummingbird. The trumpet-creeper is sometimes mistaken for the poison sumac, and has been called "cow itch"; however, its leaves have no poisonous effect at all on the skin.

Wahoo, depending entirely on which mountain family you're talking to, is also known as hearts-a-bustin' or strawberry bush. It hides there, deliberately in early summer, quiet and inconspicuous, just passing the time until autumn when its wine-colored pods open and expose their brilliant orange-red seeds.

Passion flower is the name given by early Catholic explorers who related the parts of the flower to symbols of the Crucifixion. The corona, they said, represented the crown of thorns; the stamens and pistil, the nails of the cross; the petals and sepals, the faithful apostles. And any Georgia oldtimer will tell you that a dogwood tree never grows large because it was cursed when Jesus died on a cross made from its wood; and that the redbud tree is the unluckiest tree, bewitched through all eternity, because Judas hanged himself from its limbs.

Virginia bluebells, a plant of the southern mountains, was believed to be, in ancient times, a cure for diseases of the lungs. And the wood anemone, with its delicate slender stem bearing a solitary white blossom, seems to tremble in the slightest wind. But then, *anemos* is the Greek word for wind. And mythologists like to tell the tale that anemones first grew where Venus shed tears for Adonis when her beautiful lover was killed by a wild boar. Venus, they say, changed his blood into the flower: anemone.

Throughout the Gardens, ragged strips of lichen grip the trees and fences and rocks, looking, on close examination, much like a miniature rain forest, moist and brilliant in the dead of winter, the color of freshly-cut emeralds, so tiny and fragile, yet so strong and stubborn.

One type of lichen, the British Soldier, resembles a small clump of short, grey-green stalks capped in red. Others may appear to be lettuce leaves, spanish moss, or even seashells, all in miniature.

They are small plants— half-algae and half-fungi— rootless, flowerless, and seedless. Lichens do not need soil in order to grow and thrive. Aiding the process which makes soil out of rocks is one of their ecological duties in life.

The lichens dissolve the minerals from the rocks, and their rootlike strands pry their way into the minute cracks. The rocks then crumble into small particles of soil, providing a base for other plants to grow. But it is not an overnight process. It takes a long time—not just years, but centuries and eons. Some scientists even believe that much of the soil we depend on for our very existence was probably started ages ago by those tiny, prying lichens.

Crustose lichens are thin, flaky growths on rocks and trees, resembling dried paint or pancake batter. Foliose lichens are flat, crinkled, and leaflike. It is the fruticose lichens that can pass for lettuce and spanish moss.

Stroll through the woodland and you walk lightly over the spiked sweetgum balls that have dropped and scattered at your feet. Stop for a moment at the remnants of an old hedgerow, created by man and mule when many of the 2,500 acres were under cultivation, then look out across Mountain Creek Lake, spreading through a valley that once was fenced-in cornfields.

There is a great deal to see in the Gardens, but much of it is not visible to the careless observer. It is hidden and you have to search for it. The Gardens are heavily planted and immaculately cared for, but they are like a rustic nature preserve—an environmental conservatory. They are carefully managed and highly protected, and at the same time they are natural and, in a sense—wild blending both native plants in their natural setting and many imported ornamental varieties. Beauty is easy to find.

That is the primary reason for the network of trails. There are

Spillway from Mountain Creek Lake

Black rock moss

Hardy neopolitan cyclamen

Sweetgum ball surrounded by lichens

three basic trail systems. One teaches a variety of ecological lessons, with signs and guides and a carefully printed interpretation. The second kind just identifies, names, and classifies the plants for the visitor. And the third is designed to give you a natural experience. It is closer to being a wilderness area. It is not heavily planted and there are virtually no signs. It is longer and more arduous, a gentle challenge for the outdoorsman. An amateur botanist can come in and search out the flora for himself, make his own classifications, and acquire his own personal satisfaction.

So, inspired by the vision of Cason Callaway and molded by the masters' touch of Fred Galle and his associates, the Gardens have gradually taken shape, becoming a wonderland of flora—a place where nature benevolently allows both native and foreign species to grow side by side as though they all really belonged on the same hillside instead of continents apart.

The common grey squirrel, shy fox squirrels, and spritely little chipmunks dart playfully from tree to tree, from hiding place to hiding place. Cottontail rabbits rustle through the underbrush and, in summer, muskrats slip lazily through the water of the Gardens' dozen lakes, intruding, for a season, into the slow motion world of the turtles that float and rest and sun themselves on rocks and creek banks.

Many trees, especially the bald cypress, have been scarred by the teeth marks of the beaver; some of the hidden streams far back in the woods are being dammed up again by nature's own little construction engineers.

The fox, deer, bobcat, opossum, raccoon, and mink are forgoing a life on mountainsides beyond trails, beyond the threatening footsteps of man. They prowl the peaks and call the valleys home.

Daffodils

Piedmont azalea, native

Winged seeds of red maple

Mallard under Piedmont azalea on the Wildflower Trail

*Raindrops on
golden club leaf*

Slug on shelf fungus

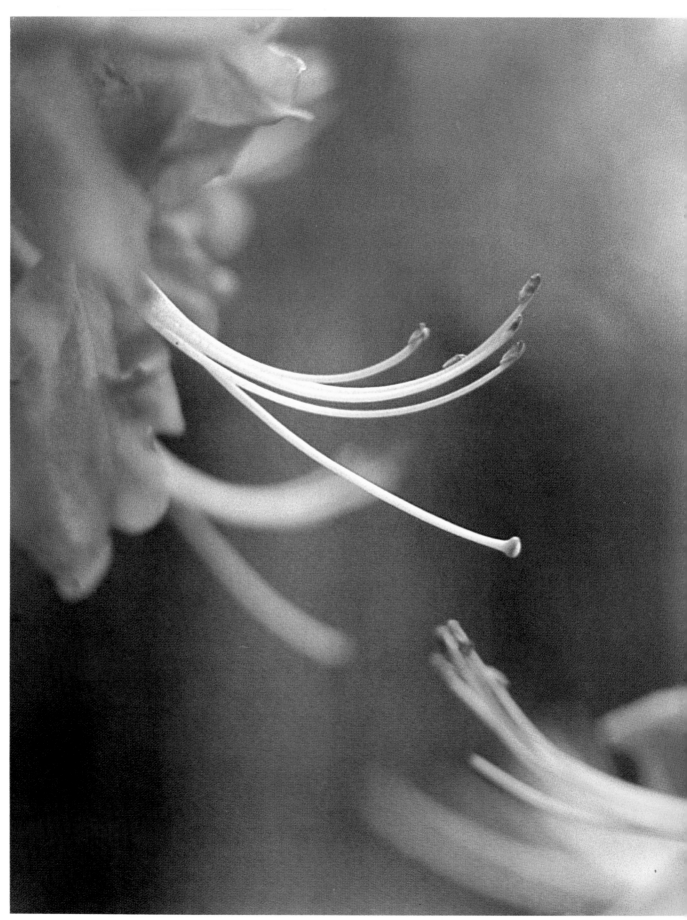

Oconee azalea, native

The Unending Season

In the darkness the Gardens sleep.

For so many years, the forest itself had slept, awaiting the hand of man to gently awaken it. Those had been the years when the land was gutted and scarred, when its banks were eroded, when its dogwood was almost exterminated because the wood made such good spindles for the area's cotton mills.

This had been the backyard horticultural world of Ben Pace and Fred Galle, the men who were given the arduous task of creating a garden showplace on a ragged floor of land gone wrong.

Pace remembers, "We spent several years going to old abandoned homesites and collecting plants like daffodils or the pseudo-narcissus that had been planted so many years ago, then deserted and forgotten.

"And we tried to take nature just as it existed, not change it. When we found native colonies of azaleas, hollies, and laurel, we didn't move them so much as we merely planted around them.

"The best compliment people pay us is when they say they can't tell which plants have been added to the woodland."

Galle and his staff are also constantly looking for areas that are being developed for housing or dams. He says, "When a bulldozer goes in to clear an area, it just cuts down and destroys—unfeeling for any plants in its path. Many times we've gotten there just in time to rescue threatened trees and flowers and to bring them safely back to the Gardens."

In the southwestern corner of South Carolina, Galle heard of a dam being built by the Army Corps of Engineers. The timber in the river bottom had been sold and was being lumbered. He knew also, that it was in this area where *Shortia,* a rare wildflower of the mountains, had its last foothold on the earth.

Oconee bells *(Shortia)* is a low, evergreen ground cover highlighted in spring by white and pink flowers. It had been collected when America was young by early French explorers and botanists. Then the wildflowers vanished. No one even remembered *Shortia* until a Harvard professor, Dr. Asa Gray, happened to see a record of them while studying an old herbarium sheet in France.

It would take Dr. Gray another 30 years of constant searching to finally rediscover them in a remote valley of South Carolina. Even then, he needed help. A young boy, hunting with his father, stumbled across the tiny flowers and, being curious, brought the leaves back to be identified. For Dr. Gray, the search had ended.

Now, once again, the threat of extinction hung over the rare mountain ground cover. So Galle and the garden staff hiked back into the valley and brought a patch of *Shortia* out, even as the bulldozers were scooping away the land around him.

Callaway Gardens also depends heavily on its propagation greenhouse for seeds and cuttings of native plants to keep the forest blooming.

The conservatory and greenhouse, with an acre of vegetation under glass, is the largest of its kind in the South, serving as a center for horticulture, education, research, and public service. Two unique observation decks provide, from an upper level, vistas of both inside and outside displays of plants in season. And wandering paths offer intimate views of plants in all the display houses.

The greenhouse has come a long way since that first potting shed of 1953, when it was used primarily for just growing and cultivating bedding plants to be used on the grounds. Now it has been carefully divided into three temperature ranges: tropical, arid, and cool. And it always has brilliant displays. Indian summer days bring out chrysanthemums, then the Christmas season offers poinsettias and cyclamen. Daffodils and tulips signal the coming of spring, along with the calceolarias, cinerarias, primulas, azaleas, and lilies. Late May and June features the tuberous begonias and fuchsias. And throughout the seasons, you can find arrangements of fern, bird-of-paradise, philodendrons, figs, anthuriums, and tropical plants that need the constant temperatures of the greenhouse for survival.

There is the *Acanthus mollis,* whose image was used by ancient Romans to decorate their scrolls, Corinthian columns, murals, and sculpture; and the crocus, the stamen of which is used as saffron, a spice for cooking in France. However, it takes 8,000 of them to make a pound, although that pound sells for $465. The desert *Aloe vera* is a member of the lily family whose sap contains the drug, aloin, which can be used effectively to heal burns. In China, it is also used in cosmetics.

The greenhouse is a year-round effort to provide an indoor showplace to brighten the winter months. The long-range hope is to put more emphasis on the greenhouse as an educational facility.

In the exhibit lobby, you can find floral art by famous artists, local Georgia crafts, photographs, or dioramas interpreting nature. The outdoor display beds, surrounding a central fountain, come alive in spring with tulips, hyacinths, flowering cherries, pansies, peonies, wallflowers, iris,and in autumn with chrysanthemums.

But it is in the work buildings, out of sight, where the real work is done. Galle says, "This is the place where every plant comes in. If we find a rare or unusual plant available from the U.S. Department of Agriculture or from some other arboretum, we request it. Then if it's hardy enough and we can successfully develop it for southern soils, we can have it ready for widespread distribution within a couple of years."

Spring display of tulips, daffodils, and azaleas in greenhouse

Coral plant

Phalaenopsis, orchid

Here in the greenhouse area is also the All-America Selection Garden for annuals. Another All-America selection facility is Mr. Cason's Vegetable Garden, those 7½ acres that Callaway dreamed would one day be "the most interesting and unusual vegetable patch in the Southeast." It was the last major project launched by Callaway before his death in 1961, and over the years, it has become an outstanding demonstration of scientific, educational, and practical application of fruit and vegetable culture.

Callaway had always considered himself an apostle of better farming. This garden was to be his final textbook. He wanted the garden planted with a wide variety of fruits and vegetables and he wished it to have the highest production of any comparable area in the country. As a living example for his neighboring farmers, he wanted to accomplish this feat by using and refining the best cultural methods including soil fertility, pest control, and crop rotation.

Cason Calloway would not have been disappointed.

Closeup of gamolepis

Gamolepis bud

The garden has become a veritable mixture of the exotic globe artichokes, chayotas, and salsifys, growing successfully alongside such familiar Georgia produce as peaches, pears, grapes, tomatoes, beans, and collards.

The lower terrace has been planted with muscadine grapes, figs, plums, peaches, persimmons, cherries, apples, and pomegranates. The middle terrace opens the year with cole crops which include lettuce, cabbage, and radishes. Then in April and May, there are patches of tomatoes, corn, beans, squash, okra, and peppers. With the arrival of fall, you can find rows of cauliflower, broccoli, and brussels sprouts.

The 3-acre upper terrace has been reserved especially for bunch grapes, bramble fruits, strawberries, blueberries, and herbs. There is the sweet basil, "to make a man merry and glad," and rosemary, "for remembrance." Dill is hung in the house to protect against evil spirits. And fennel, horehound, spearmint, applemint, peppermint, and oregano have been sown merely to enhance their medicinal, culinary, and aromatic reputations.

Callaway, as one of the nation's 26 All-America Selection Gardens, takes new, unnamed varieties of vegetables each year and grows them to be evaluated and compared with standard varieties.

Horticulturists, over the past few decades, have become more and more like that unique breed of individualists called art collectors. Rather than selling their valuable flowers when—for some reason or other—they no longer have use for them, they are willing or donating their collections to responsible arboretums and gardens throughout the country.

One of the prize gifts to Callaway Gardens is the famed Kurume azalea collection of the John Ames family of Boston. That race of azalea was originated by a Japanese, Motozo Sakamoto, who lived in the city of Kurume, on the southern island of Kyushu, during the early part of the 19th century. Parents of the species had come from the slopes of the sacred Kirishima-yama, a volcanic mountain. They grow there, still in abundance in the volcanic soil, across the grassy slopes, and among the rocks.

But it was not until 1914 that botanist E. H. Wilson found these azaleas a few miles north of Tokyo and became amazed at the purity of their color, varying from pink to rose, lavender, magenta, salmon, deep scarlet, and white. Three years later he journeyed to Kurume to further investigate this intriguing azalea. And he said, "The gardens were veritable fairylands, and I gasped with astonishment when I realized that garden-lovers of America and Europe knew virtually nothing of this wealth of beauty."

In 1917, Wilson persuaded John Ames to introduce the collection to the United States, and he returned from his Japanese wanderings with a group of plants called "The Wilson 50." None of the original plants are left today, but many of the azaleas in the Ames gardens are direct descendents.

Galle had long been searching for remnants of the Wilson 50 and began a correspondence with Oliver Ames of Boston. After two or three letters, he received word: "How would you like to have the whole collection for your Gardens?"

Ames had kept the plants in an old conservatory, but now his gardener was retiring. Maintenance was much too difficult for his personal liking. And Boston winters, he admitted, were too cold for azaleas. So the plants arrived at Callaway Gardens, 200 of them, in a 42-foot van. Eight of them were rare.

Oddly enough, a Japanese family, the Domotos, were bringing the Kurume azalea to San Francisco about the same time that Wilson was returning in 1917. Only 2 years earlier, a gold medal had been awarded to 30 of the plants at San Francisco's Panama-Pacific Exposition.

Galle spent almost 3 years corresponding with the last of the Domoto family, receiving promises that he would have some of the azaleas as a donation. At last, Galle headed for San Francisco to talk with the 70-year-old son. And 2 weeks later, he finally had parts of the whole collection.

He says, "We still don't have a whole set of Wilson's 50 species. But thanks to a gathering of the East and the West, we're coming closer."

Ilex wilsonii, a native of China and one of the rare hollies in the world, was also brought back by an exploring E. H. Wilson. Some seedlings were given to an old friend of Galle's, Ernest Morrell, after the initial planting in the Arnold Arboretum in Boston. They became lost (rather than banned) in Boston. And Galle suddenly realized a few years ago that there were only two of the original plants left in the world. They both belonged to Morrell. They both were willed to Callaway Gardens.

Galle talks of the J.G.C. Bloodworth Collection of azaleas and rhododendrons, the culmination of a lifelong work by a fellow Georgian in Atlanta. His garden rolled magnificently over 40 acres and was immaculate.

When Galle and Pace heard of Bloodworth's death, they drove to visit with the amateur horticulturist's daughter, offering their help. Galle had hoped that the large manicured garden could be left intact and could become a flowering showplace for Atlanta. He knew the plants there were much too valuable to be destroyed or neglected.

Galle contacted several universities to see if they wanted the plants, but they were uninterested. He spoke with county and city officials, but they rejected his suggestion that the gardens be incorporated into a park.

Then one morning he received an urgent telephone call from Bloodworth's daughter. "You have 10 days to move the plants from the garden," she said. "The property has been sold and they're planning a subdivision where the garden now stands."

It was July and not the right month to transplant the shrubs and flowers. But Galle had no choice. He headed north toward Atlanta, and within the allotted 10 days had returned with 200 of the most colorful, unusual, and valuable species.

The final important donation came from Conrad Bucker of Maitland, Florida: an extremely rare collection of tropical plants, now housed in the greenhouse, that Bucker had gathered while working in the faraway regions of South America and Africa.

In 65 B.C., Horace Flaccus prayed for "a piece of land, not so very large, which would contain a garden, and near the house a spring of everflowing water, and beyond these a bit of wood."

He could easily have been praying for Callaway Gardens, a land whose best fertilizer had been the footprints of its owners. For when no land existed, they weren't afraid to try to create it, especially if it were to be a refuge for the comical little coots and the emerald-hooded mallards that rule jointly over the pine-walled lakes.

One fear had been that too many of the helpless ducks were losing the game of survival to woodland foxes. They needed a place of escape, so a little island was built in the middle of Hummingbird Lake — a private, personal refuge for waterfowl. But dirt would not stay, so an island of Styrofoam was finally constructed, covered with sod and grass and rocks and native hypericum. It looked real. And, surprisingly enough, it didn't float away.

But the muskrats came and ate the hypericum. Now the only plant growing on the little artificial island is a self-sown willow tree, the way nature meant for it to be.

Neither gardens nor gardeners ever rest. The life cycle goes on. And man is given two choices. He can either work to help improve the land where the flowers grow, or he can misuse the soil and severely stunt the development of a forest. At Callaway Gardens, man has joined hands with the vibrant thrust of nature, enriching the earth and creating a protective monument to the delicate life of the surprising woodland.

For a time, sleep may come to parts of the Gardens. But the miracle of the seasons is never silenced nor diminished. The winter is grey, interlaced with evergreen foliage and the red and yellow berries of the hollies. Springtime ushers brilliance to the limbs of azalea and rhododendron, and subtle softness to the petals of redbud and dogwood. In summer, the valleys are ablaze with the quiltwork designs of wildflower patches. And autumn is a frosty explosion of red and gold dappled with splashes of chrysanthemums.

Quietly, behind the scenes, horticulture experts diligently work in greenhouses, on mountain slopes, in ravines, and in vegetable gardens, searching for the perfect species. Some have already been found. But no horticulturist ever allows himself the luxury of total satisfaction.

Kurume azaleas

According to Hal Northrup, "The need to develop a location where people retreat for relaxation, learning, inspiration, natural beauty, and wholesome recreation is becoming increasingly important to our society. As we plan for the future, this quality will continue to be the dominant direction of Callaway Gardens. The founders' objective to take nothing from the Gardens except nourishment for the soul, consolation for the heart, and inspiration for the mind remains our intent."

The cycle of nature never ceases. And neither does the experimental work of man at the Gardens.

Together the search goes on, hand in hand, in perfect harmony through the days and the nights of an unending season.

Crocus pistil in closeup

Crocus bulb

Lichens on crab apple branch   *English ivy*

Dew on Christmas fern

Cinerarias in greenhouse

Leaves of velvet plant

Dew on crocus

Red Robin azalea, Kurume

Rhododendron bud

Crab apple trees in bloom

Piedmont azalea against loblolly pine

Canada geese facing west on Mountain Creek Lake

Shepherd
of the
Lake

In the east the sky is grey, the color of lead, and streaked with ragged threads of blue. In the west, it is pink — turning orange — and the sun has not yet touched the treetops that reach up from the hillside. The lake is white, like marble, in late evening beneath the shadows of the pine. Within minutes, it will be golden, then purple, as another day slips away from the Georgia Piedmont.

Above, a graceful "V" of mallards angles into the lake from their thermal over the eastern shore. A breeze, like a sigh, rustles the holly. Fourteen mallards glide in for a landing, slicing the water gently, and leaving a long, thin ripple behind them. One honks. Even the aristocratic Canadian geese are happy.

Coots bob like tiny black dots on the water — black dots with scarlet eyes. They sail toward shore in miniature convoys, staggered, yet all together, as though searching for an unseen destination at the foot of the pines.

The soft veil of evening hangs like lace above the water. The mallards have become patches of black in a darkening sky. One flies alone. Another honks from the water. And that solitary figure high above the treetops sweeps suddenly upward, then veers sharply to the left, flattening his wings against the grey of the east before sailing with that summer wind, gliding in and out of the shadows of the forest, back into the bosom of the calling water.

He drops with the grace and the silence of a single feather, nestling into the comfort of the lake that is home, where his friends are waiting. And, for a time, he is not alone anymore.

The red has vanished behind the hilltops, leaving its last, pink goodbye to the day. The sky is the color of peaches now. And the snow geese and mallards and coots head into the dark of the western end of the lake.

One great Canadian goose will lead them. He is called Oscar. He is the shepherd of his flock who watches darkness come into the valley to steal away the daylight, who knows when the last flame of twilight will flicker — then die — draping the lake in that transparent black velvet of evening.

Canada geese on Mountain Creek Lake after dark

Drake mallard in flight

Oscar has spent his day wrapped in summer sunshine, often standing alone on the grassy point just beyond the golf clubhouse. The coots have played and splashed at the water's edge, and the mallards have disappeared into the brush and marshland of the tiny coves wedged back out of sight along the meandering shoreline.

The Canadian geese have flocked around Oscar, treading on his solitude and not wishing to leave his side. He occasionally leads them for long, easy spins around Mountain Creek Lake. They stretch out single file and float like great feathered statues, alive, buoyant as hope, kicking water, yet leaving no trail to mark their path — no ripple as evidence they have even been there.

But for most of his daylight hours, Oscar stands motionless on the point. Waiting.

During the day he watches the coots and mallards ignore him as they frolic with wild abandon in the summer-warm water. Now, it is the coming of night; they need him to lead them to the sundown side of the lake. Some are missing, as some always are; he will look for them, making sure none of the birds face the darkness alone.

The geese and coots and mallards have begun their westward swim across the orange of the water. Its brilliance is fading; all that is left is a single thread of gold where the last ray of sunlight has touched, then pierced the cotton candy surface of the lake.

The Canadian geese, in single file again, ease across that lone golden thread, cutting it for a moment, and blotting out the red of the low sun, holding for

Canada goose on sunset water

Canada geese at twilight

one last look across the horizon before dropping below the other side of the world.

Oscar lifts his graceful black neck, ruffles his feathers, and makes his last flight to the empty far corner of the lake.

He lands, then begins his day's final journey alone, leaving soft, rippling creases in the water behind him, honking wildly, calling for the lost; searching frantically in hidden inlets, and finding the strays; looking very

much like a tired old cowhand chasing down calves at the end of the day.

The unforgotten gather behind him. They move quickly beneath, then beyond, an empty bridge and sail unseen into the great reach of night.

The pale, granite water has turned to ink.